ABC

Musical Instruments from The Metropolitan Museum of Art

Florence Cassen Mayers

Harry N. Abrams, Inc.
Publishers
New York

For my sister, Lois, and for Martin, Lisa, and Adam

Editor: Harriet Whelchel
Designer: Florence Cassen Mayers
Picture and Caption Research: The staff of the departments of Musical
                              Instruments and Special Publications at
                              The Metropolitan Museum of Art
Photography: The Metropolitan Museum of Art Photograph Studio

Library of Congress Cataloging-in-Publication Data
Mayers, Florence Cassen.
ABC : musical instruments from the Metropolitan Museum of Art/
Florence Cassen Mayers.
     p.   cm.
Summary: Presents a variety of musical instruments from the collection of the
Metropolitan Museum in alphabetical order.
ISBN 0–8109–1878–1 : $9.95
1. Musical instruments—Catalogs and collections—New York (N.Y.)—Juvenile
literature. 2. Metropolitan Museum of Art (New York, N.Y.)—Catalogs—Juvenile
literature. [1. Musical instruments. 2. Metropolitan Museum of Art (New York,
N.Y.) 3. Museums. 4. Alphabet.] I. Metropolitan Museum of Art (New York, N.Y.)
II. Title.
ML462.N5M15 1988
781.91′074′01471—dc 19
[E]   88–3336
           CIP
        MN AC

Design copyright © 1988 Florence Cassen Mayers
Photographs copyright © 1988 The Metropolitan Museum of Art

A Times Mirror Company

Printed and bound in Japan

Other Books in the ABC Series
ABC: Museum of Fine Arts, Boston
ABC: The Museum of Modern Art, New York
ABC: The National Air and Space Museum
ABC: Egyptian Art from The Brooklyn Museum
ABC: Costume and Textiles from the Los Angeles County
     Museum of Art

Title page:
Chwago (Drum), c. 1982
Kyung Suk Park, South Korean
Wood, canvas, metal, and hide; 51¾″ high
Gift of Korean Cultural Service, 1982   1982.171.8

Introduction

In this unique ABC book, each letter of the alphabet is illustrated with one or more selections from the extraordinary collection of musical instruments in The Metropolitan Museum of Art, New York. The collection is one of the largest of its kind in the world, covering six continents and spanning four thousand years.

Gathered here are outstanding examples of familiar European and American instruments, and exotic non-Western ones as well. Though even the youngest child will recognize piano, drum, and others, many of the instruments will be new to children of all ages. Each can be placed in one of three basic categories: string instruments, such as the electric guitar, the mandolin, the Senegalese kora, and the Indian sarinda; wind instruments, which include the accordion, a Scottish bagpipe, the French horn, and the Peruvian quena; and percussion instruments, represented by various drums and gongs, as well as a Hawaiian ipu and a Javanese saron slen tem.

This beautiful and unusual ABC book offers young children an introduction to language, the world of music, and one of the many wonderful collections of The Metropolitan Museum of Art.

Aa

Accordion

Accordion, 20th century
Soprani Inc., Italian
Metal, wood, leather, mother-of-pearl, and rhinestones;
20⅜″ high, 29″ wide (open)
Gift of Mrs. Elias Gatz Wexner, 1969   69.42

Bb

Bagpipe

Bagpipe, 19th century
Robert MacKinnon, Scottish (Glasgow), active 1887–1902
Wood, ivory, horn, and cloth; chanter 13″ long, longest drone 32″
The Crosby Brown Collection of Musical Instruments, 1889
89.4.863

Cc

Clarinets

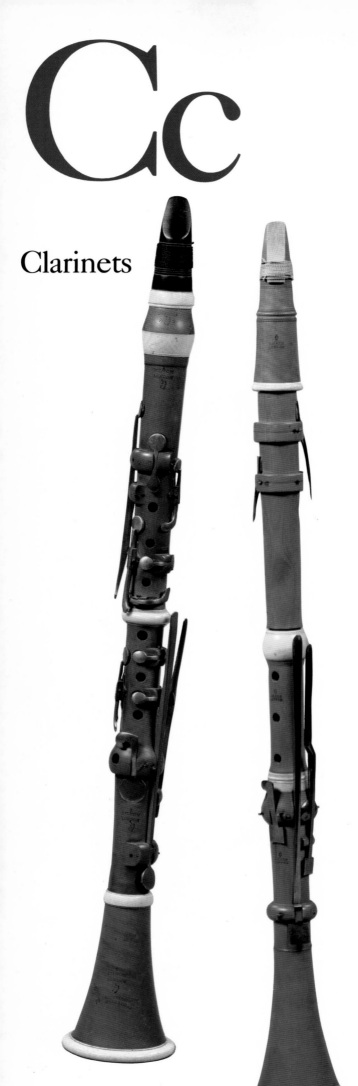

Clarinet in C
Richard John Bilton, English (London), active 1826–56;
mouthpiece by Charles Pace, English (London), active 1834–54
Wood, ivory, and brass; 23″ long
The Crosby Brown Collection of Musical Instruments, 1889
89.4.2559

Clarinet in C
John Hale, English (London), active 1784–1804
Wood, ivory, brass, and leather; 23″ long
Purchase, Funds from various donors, 1976   1976.7.7

Cornet

Cornet in B Flat, c. 1900
European
Silver-plated brass; 12⅜″ long
Purchase, Anonymous Gift, 1977   1977.246.1 a–d

Dd

Drum (O'Daiko), 19th century
Japanese
Cloisonné enamel, silk, and hide; 62⅝″ high
The Crosby Brown Collection of Musical Instruments, 1889
89.4.1236

Drums

Drum
Vili people, Loango, French Congo
Carved and painted wood; 32″ high
The Crosby Brown Collection of Musical Instruments, 1889
89.4.1743

Ee

Electric guitar

Electric Guitar, 1973–74
Bruce BecVar, American, born 1953
Various woods and other materials, including wire and
mother-of-pearl; 39⅛″ long
Gift of Arthur N. BecVar, 1980   1980.544a

Ff

French horns

Hunting Horn, late 18th–early 19th century
French (?)
Glazed pottery; 17″ long
The Crosby Brown Collection of Musical Instruments, 1889
89.4.1115

French Horn in F
J. L. Allen, American, active in New York 1864–70
Brass and nickel silver; 16⅛″ long
The Crosby Brown Collection of Musical Instruments, 1889
89.4.2198

Gg

Gong

Gong, late 19th century
Japanese, Kyoto
Carved and painted wood and metal; figures 66″ high
The Crosby Brown Collection of Musical Instruments, 1889
89.4.2016

Hh

Harpsichord

Harpsichord, 1909
Chickering and Sons (Boston), under the direction of
Arnold Dolmetsch, British, 1858–1940
Wood and other materials; 35½″ high
Gift of Mr. and Mrs. Richard H. Dana, 1981   1981.374

Ii

Ipu

Ipu, late 19th century
Hawaiian
Gourds and cloth; 30″ high
The Crosby Brown Collection of Musical Instruments, 1889
89.4.754

Jj

Jingling Johnnie

Kk

Kora

Kora, c. 1960
Mamadou Kouyaté, Senegalese
Gourd, wood, sheepskin, and metal; 45¾″ long
Rogers Fund, 1975   1975.59

L1

Lute

Lute, 1726
Gregori Ferdinand Wenger, German (Augsburg)
Wood; 31½″ long
The Crosby Brown Collection of Musical Instruments, 1889
89.4.3140

Mm

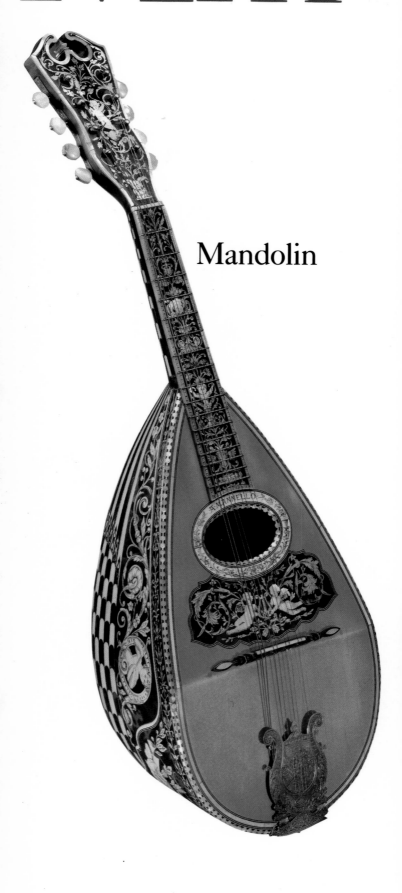

Mandolin

Mandolin, c. 1900
Angelo Mannello, Italian-born American, active 1858–1922
Wood, tortoiseshell, ivory, and metal; 24½″ long
Gift of family of Angelo Mannello, 1972   1972.111.1

Nn

Nyckelharpa

Nyckelharpa, 19th century
Swedish
Pine and other materials; 33″ long
The Crosby Brown Collection of Musical Instruments, 1889
89.4.957

Oboe

Oboe in C
Paolo del Maino, Italian (Milan), active 1830–80
Wood and nickel silver; 21¾″ long
Purchase, The Crosby Brown Collection of Musical
Instruments, by exchange, 1979   1979.296

Pp

Piano

Upright (Cabinet) Piano, 1835
Firth, Hall, and Pond, active 1832–47, American (New York)
Mahogany, ebony, and other woods; metal, and ivory; 84⅞″ high
Gift of Miss Justine M. Watson, 1944   44.57

Qq

Quena

Quena (Flute)
Peruvian, possibly Pre-Columbian
Metal and fabric; 3⅞″ long
Rogers Fund, 1981   1981.51

Rr

Rattle

Raven Rattle, 19th century
North American Indian (Tsimshian or Haida people),
British Columbia
Wood, pebbles, and paint; 13″ long
The Crosby Brown Collection of Musical Instruments, 1889
89.4.615

Ss

Sarinda

Sarinda, 19th century
Indian
Wood, parchment, and ivory; 28″ long
Gift of Miss Alice Getty, 1946   46.34.42

Saxophone

Saron slen tem

Alto Saxophone in E Flat, late 19th century
Arsène-Zoé Lecomte and Co., French (Paris)
Brass and wood; 24¼″ long
The Crosby Brown Collection of Musical Instruments, 1889
89.4.2170

Saron Slen Tem, 19th century
Javanese
Carved wood and iron; 36″ high
The Crosby Brown Collection of Musical Instruments, 1889
89.4.1462

Tt

Trumpet

Alto Trumpet in E Flat, c. 1700
I. W. Haas, German (Nuremberg), 1649–1723
Silver; 28″ long
Purchase, Funds from various donors, 1954   54.32.1

Uu

Udu pots

Udu Pots, 1985 (left) and 1984 (right), based on Nigerian models
Frank Giorgini, American, born 1947
Clay and rattan; 12½″ high (left) and 14⅛″ high (right)
Gift of Mr. and Mrs. Frank Giles Giorgini, 1985   1985.202.1–2

Vv

Violin

Violin, 1691
Antonius Stradivarius, Italian (Cremona), 1644–1737
Maple, pine, pearwood, and ebony; 23¼″ long
Gift of George Gould, 1955   55.86

Ww

Walking stick instruments

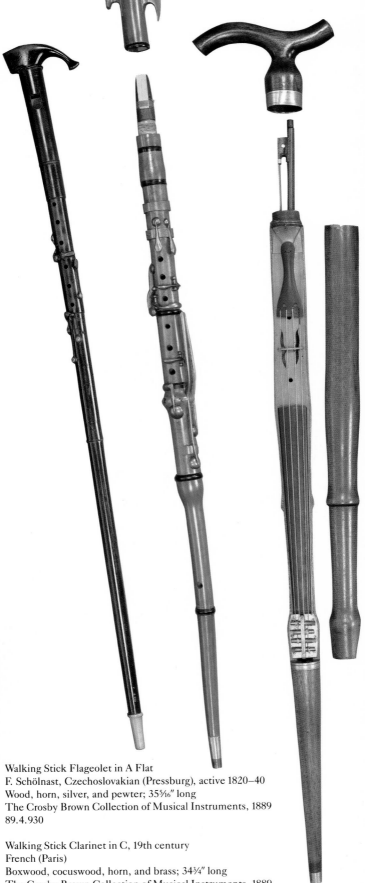

Walking Stick Flageolet in A Flat
F. Schölnast, Czechoslovakian (Pressburg), active 1820–40
Wood, horn, silver, and pewter; 35⁵⁄₁₆″ long
The Crosby Brown Collection of Musical Instruments, 1889
89.4.930

Walking Stick Clarinet in C, 19th century
French (Paris)
Boxwood, cocuswood, horn, and brass; 34¾″ long
The Crosby Brown Collection of Musical Instruments, 1889
89.4.2165

Cane Violin, 19th century
Gläsel Moritz (?), German
Various woods; 35″ long
The Crosby Brown Collection of Musical Instruments, 1889
89.4.950

Xx

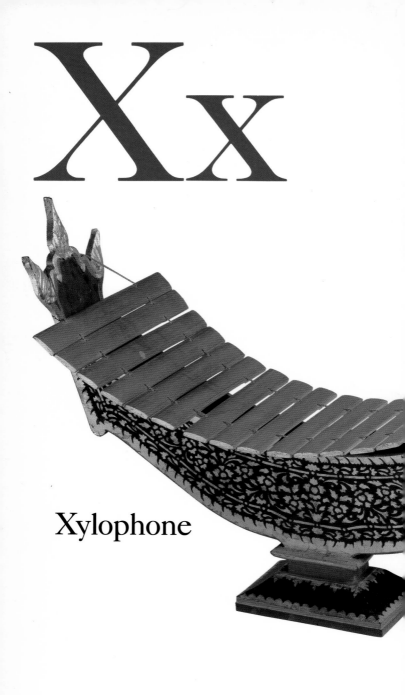

Xylophone

Yy

Yunluo

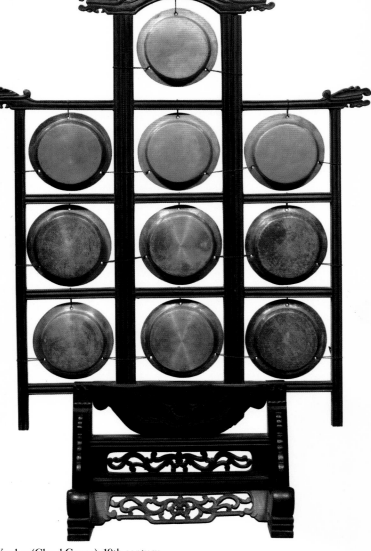

Yunluo (Cloud Gongs), 19th century
Chinese
Metal and wood; 28″ high, largest gong 4″ wide
The Crosby Brown Collection of Musical Instruments, 1889
89.4.15

Zz

Zither

Zither, late 19th century
I. Lambert, French (Val d'Ajol)
Wood and metal; 23″ long
The Crosby Brown Collection of Musical Instruments, 1889
89.4.991